Portrait #5 (2)
Portrait #1 (1)
The performance
Man with child
Portrait #4
Girl in shirt
Model III (2016)
Portrait #1 (3)
Portrait #2 (2)
Figure
Portrait #2 (3)
Portrait #5 (4)
Portrait #4

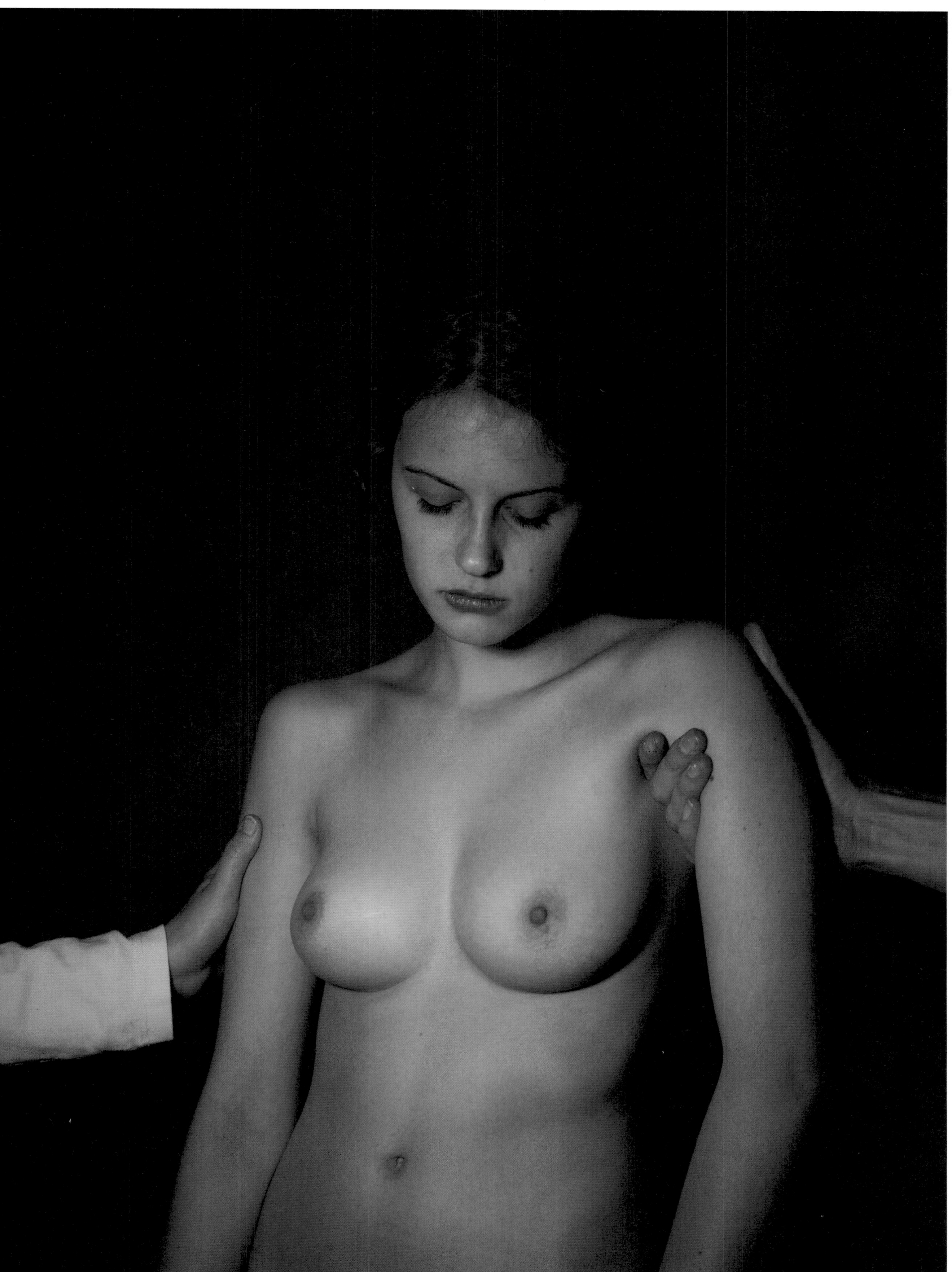

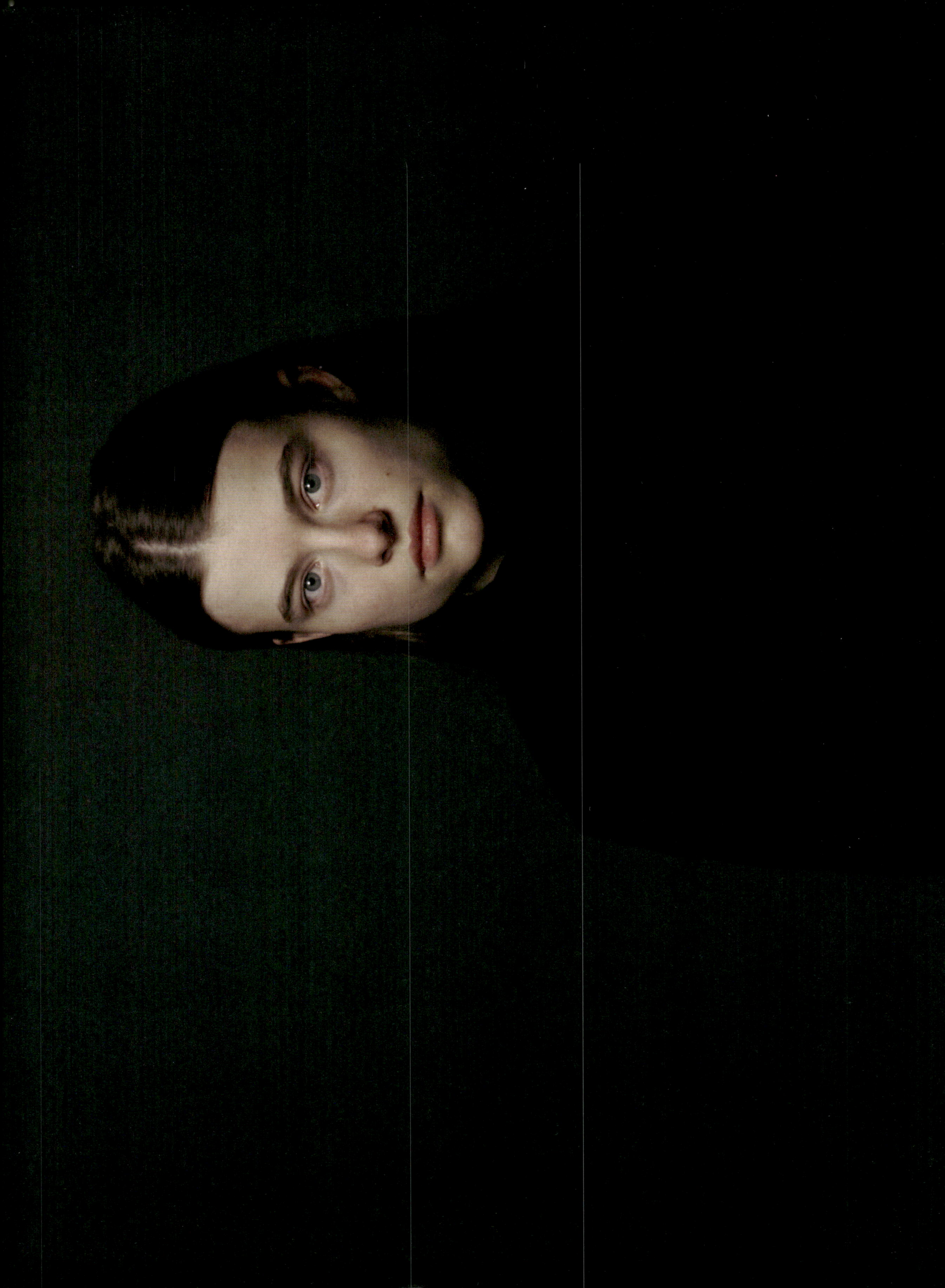

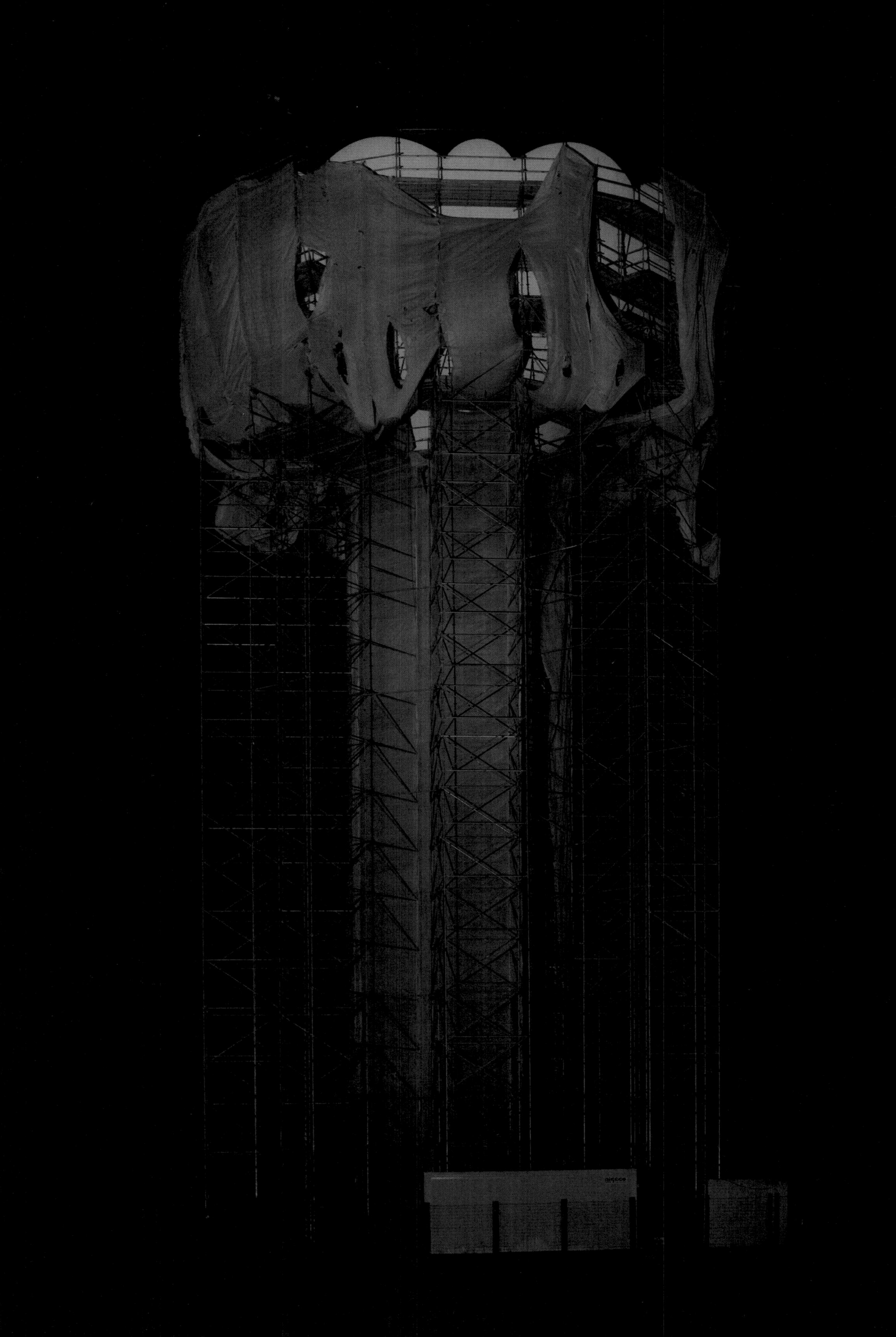

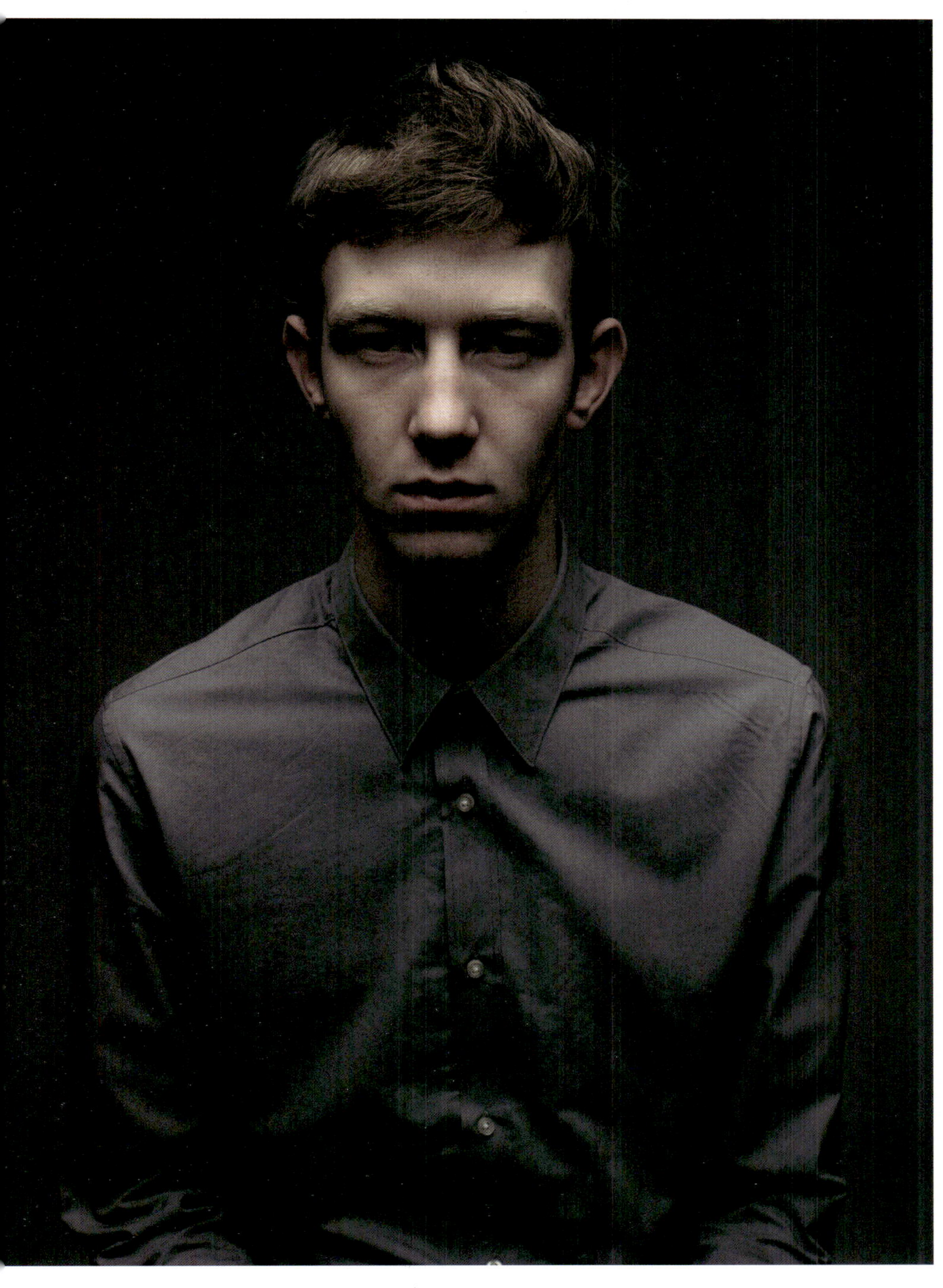

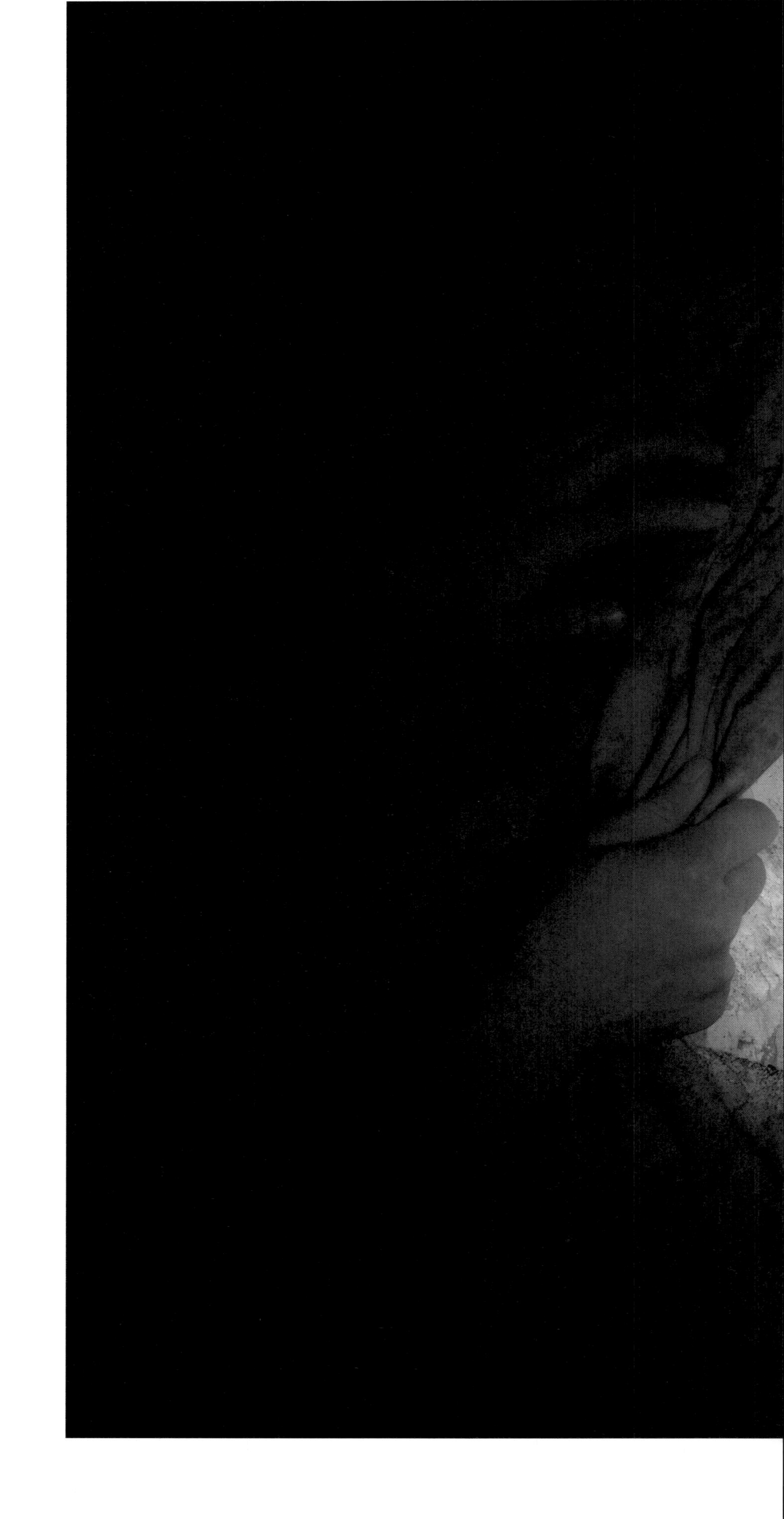

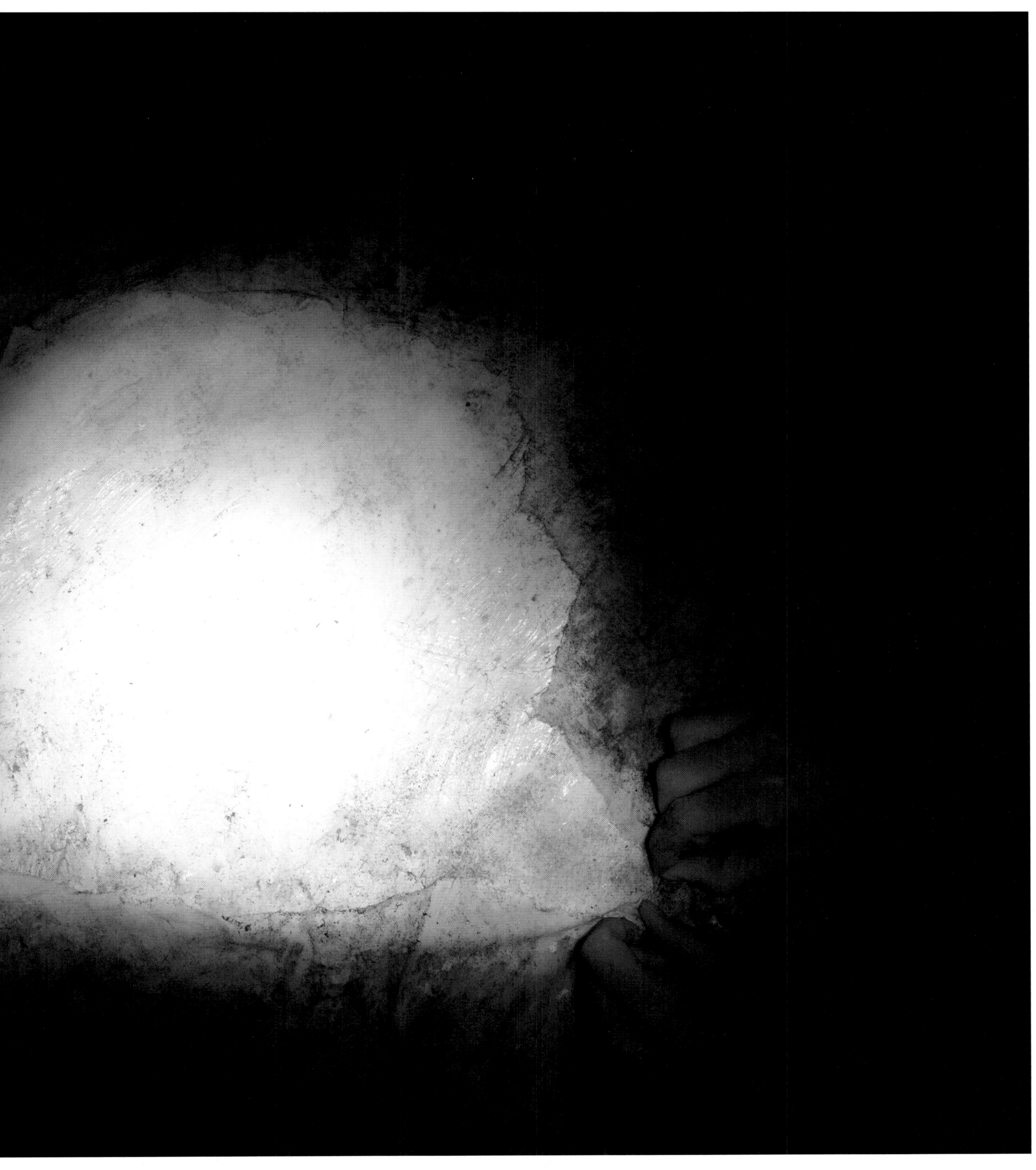

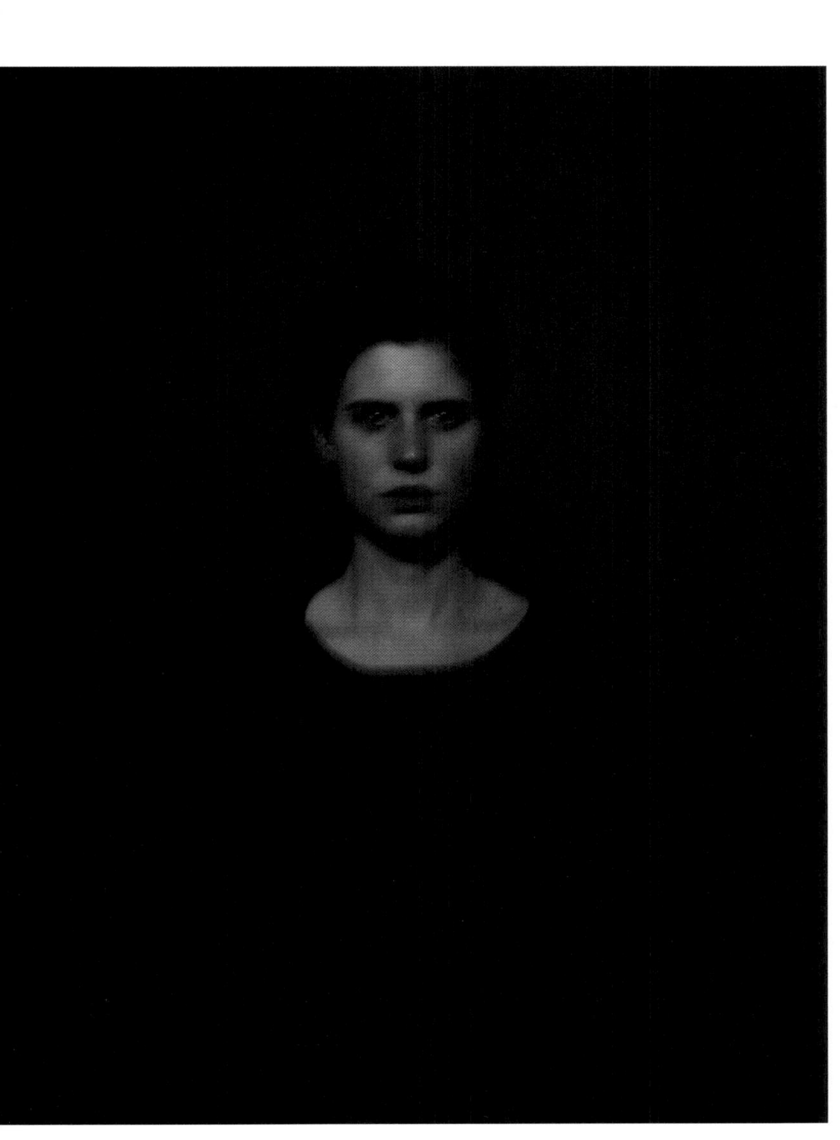

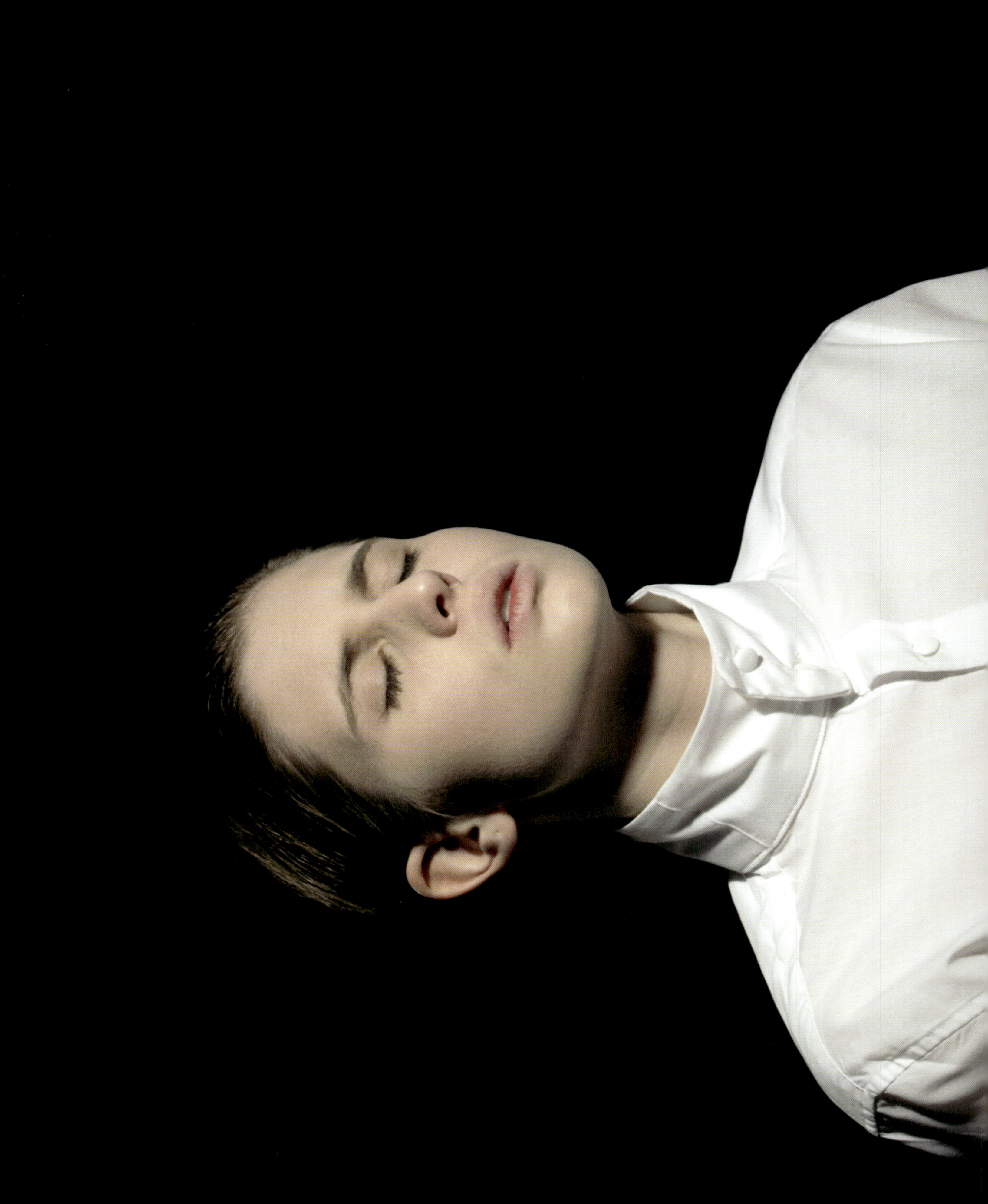

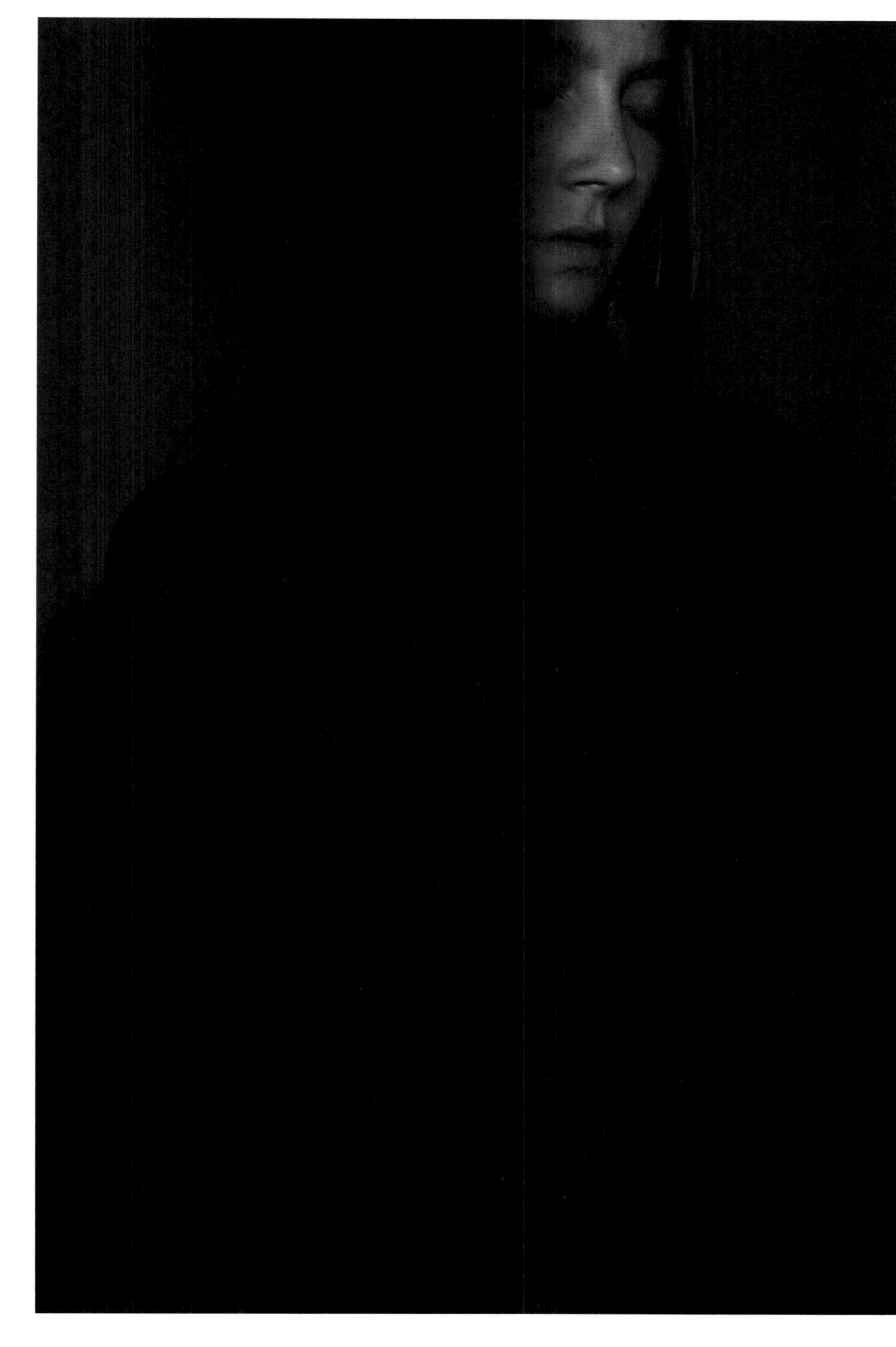

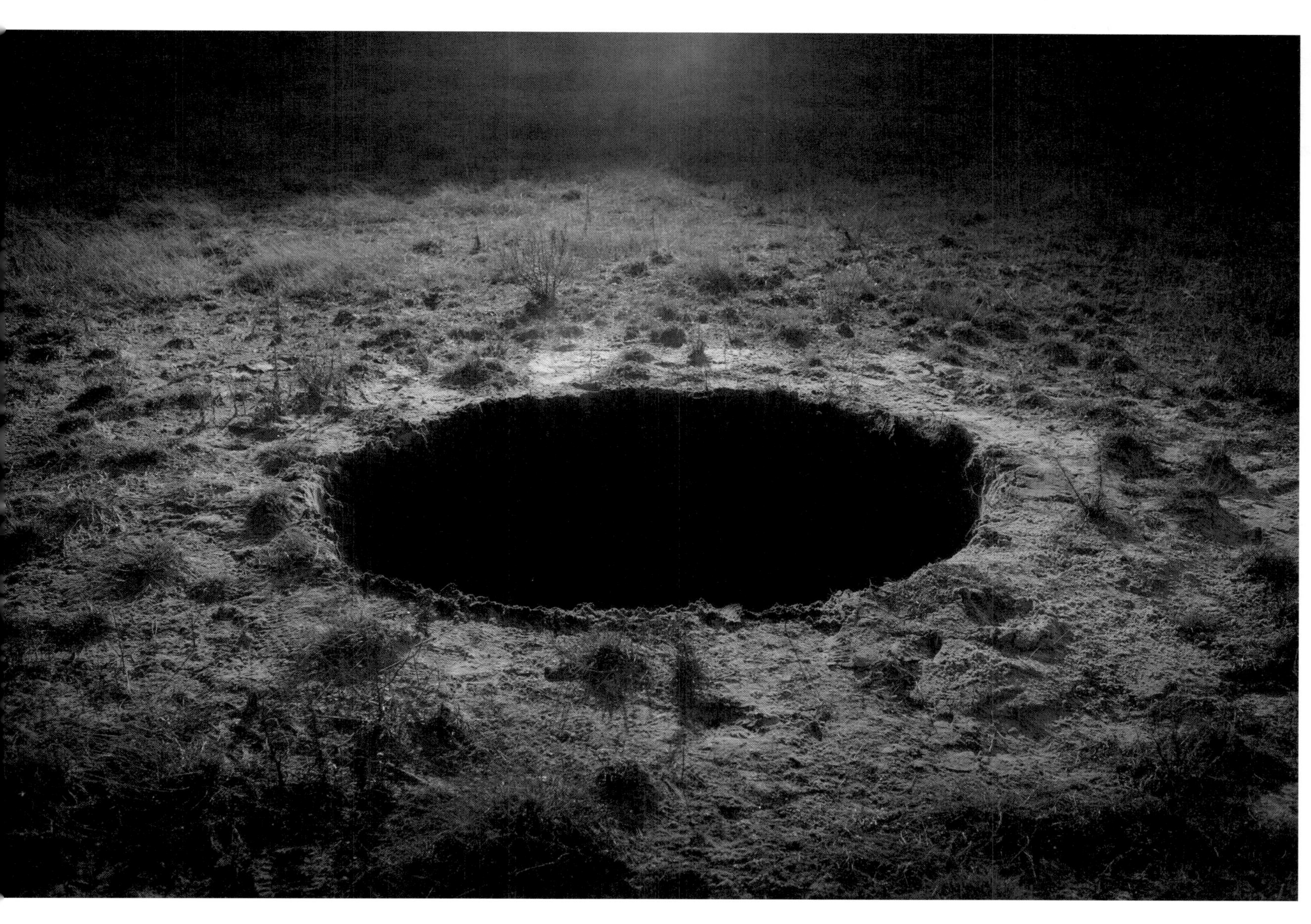

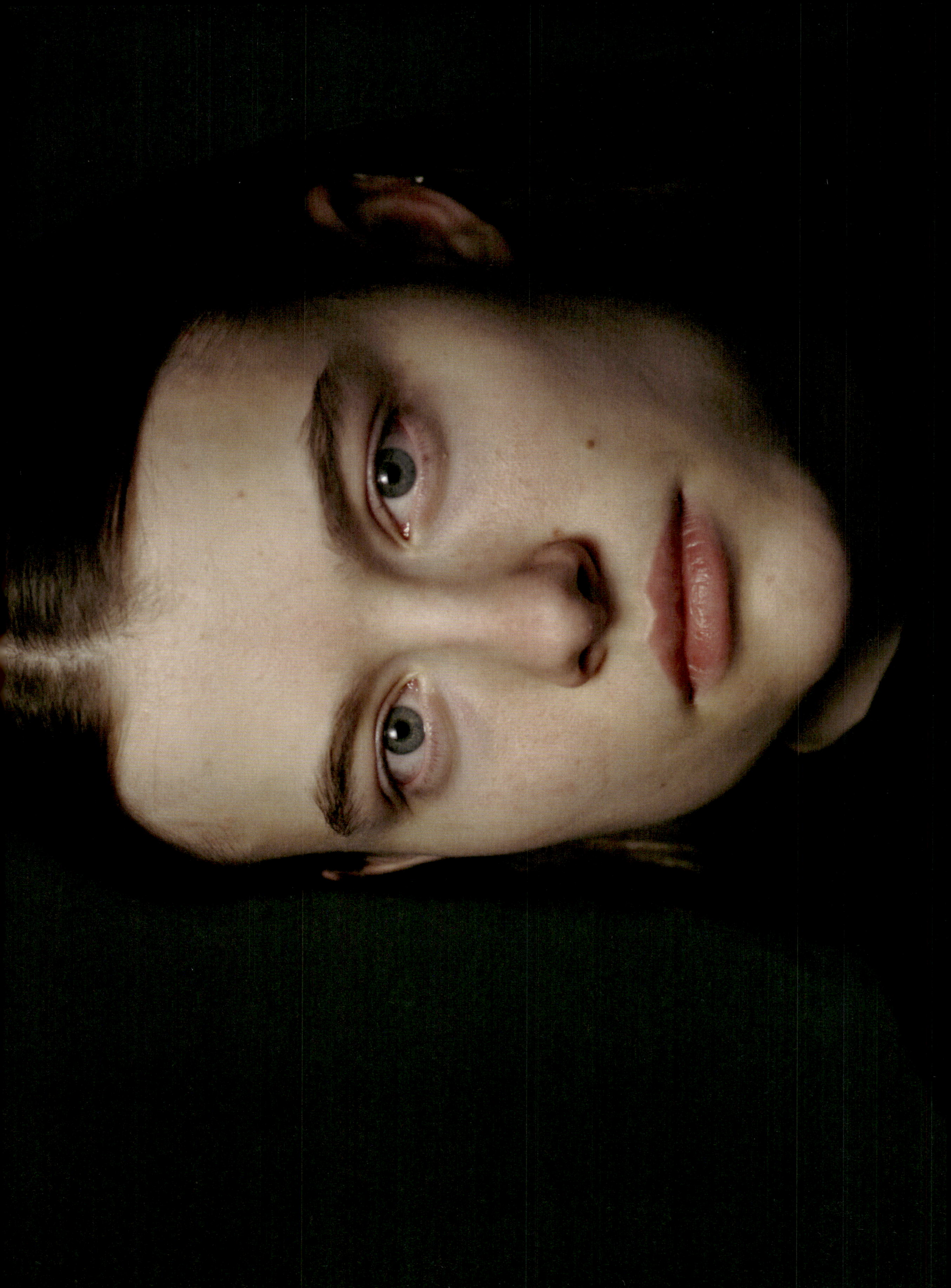

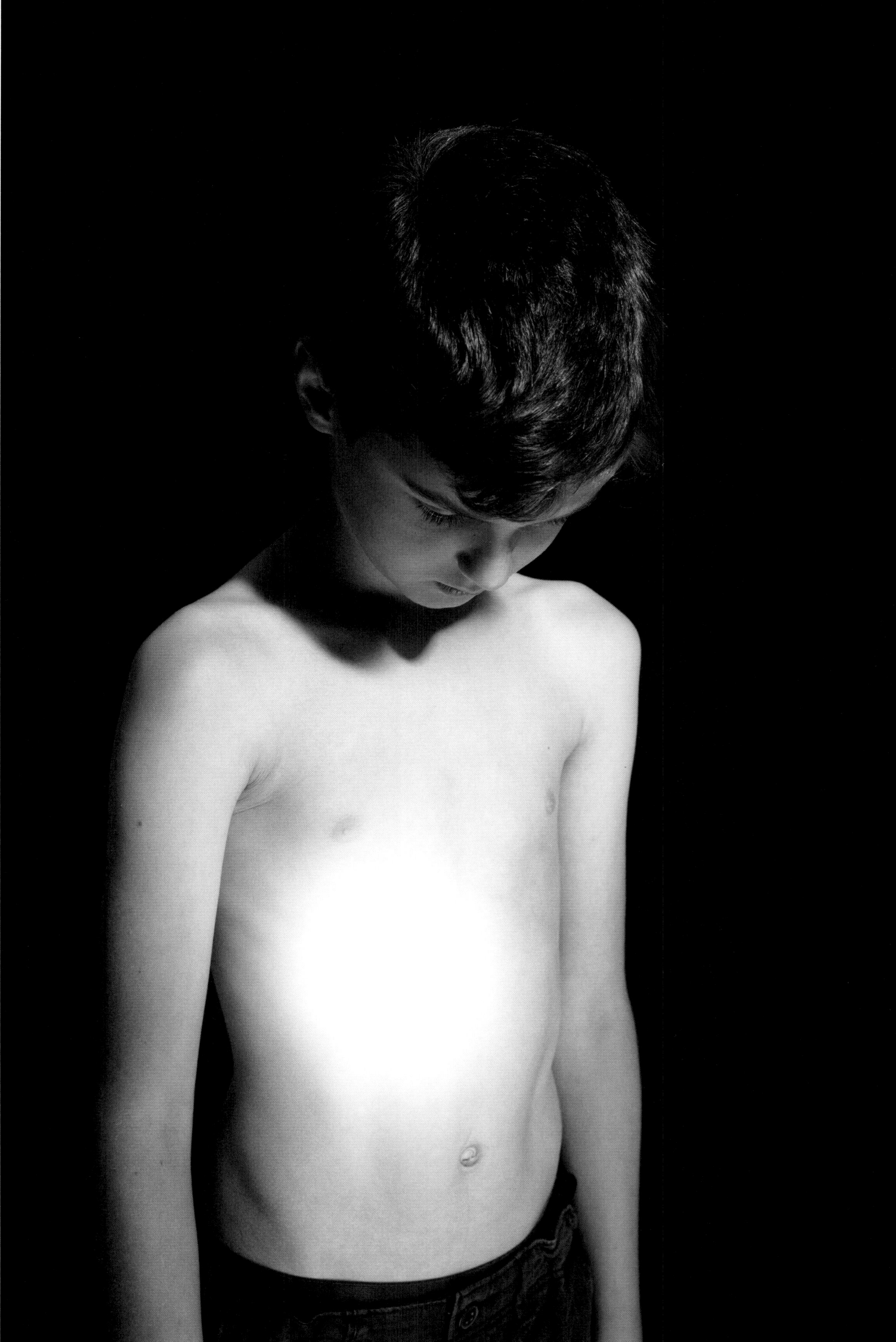

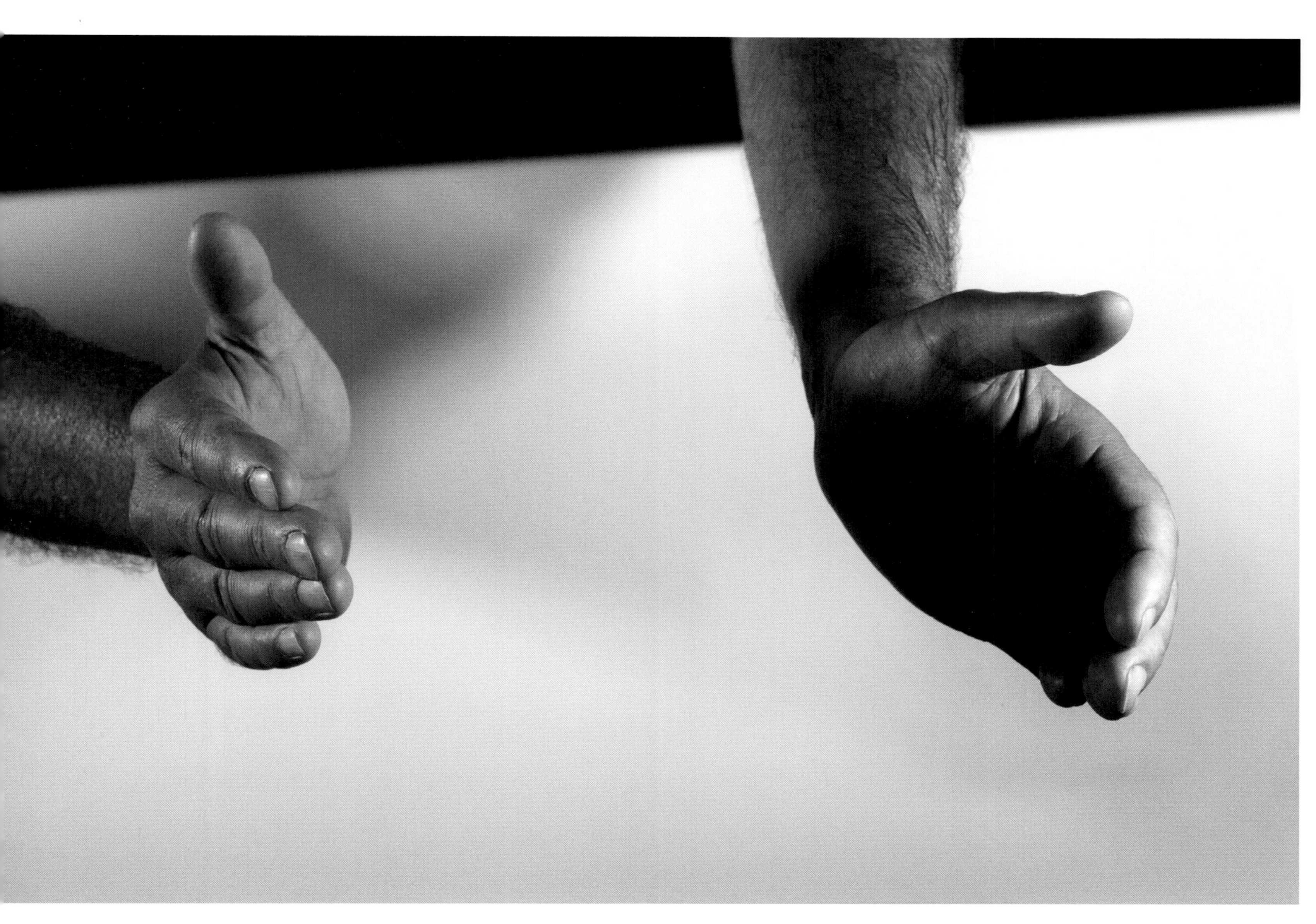

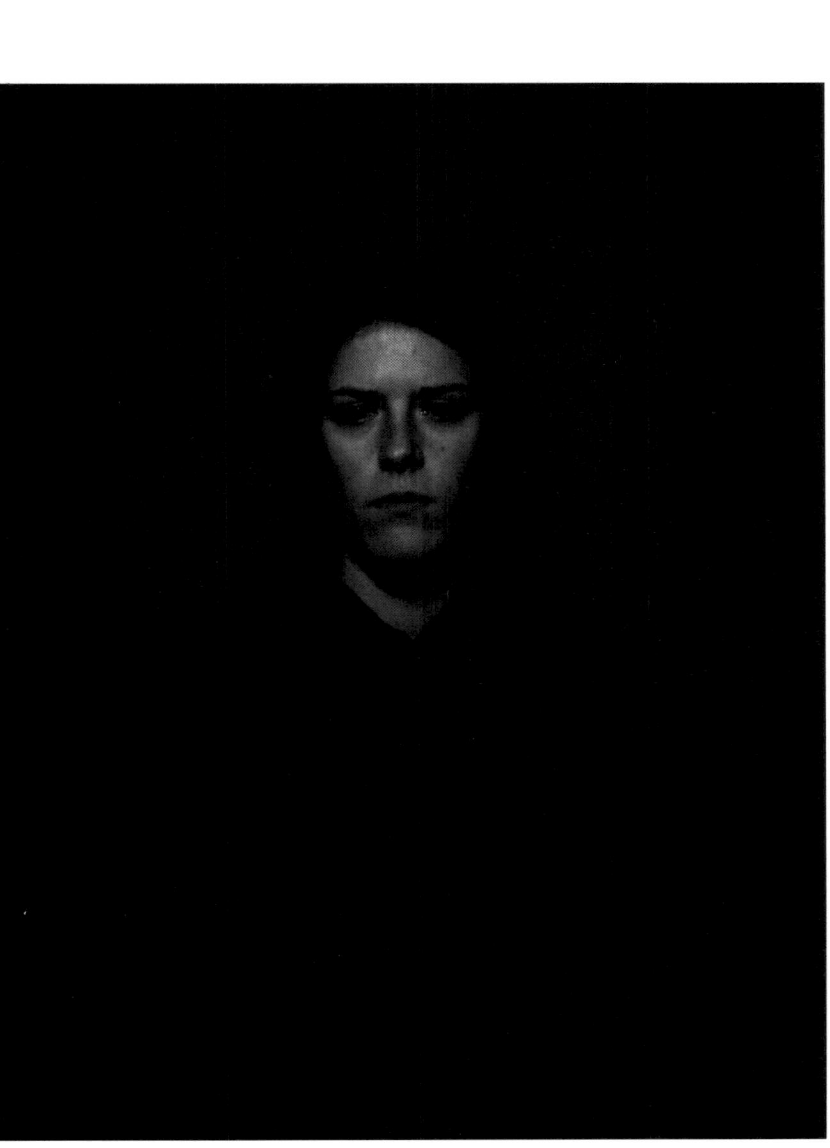

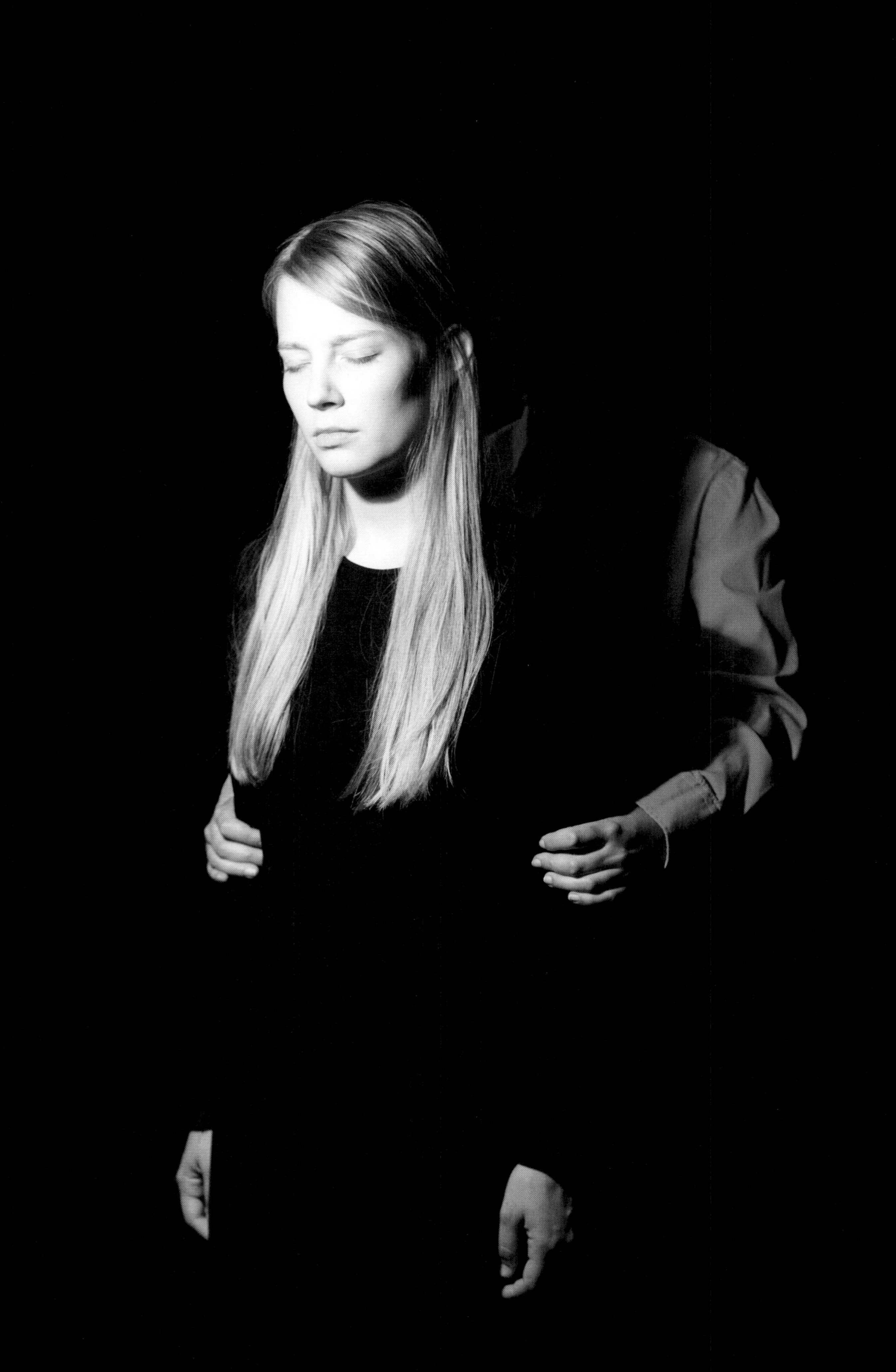

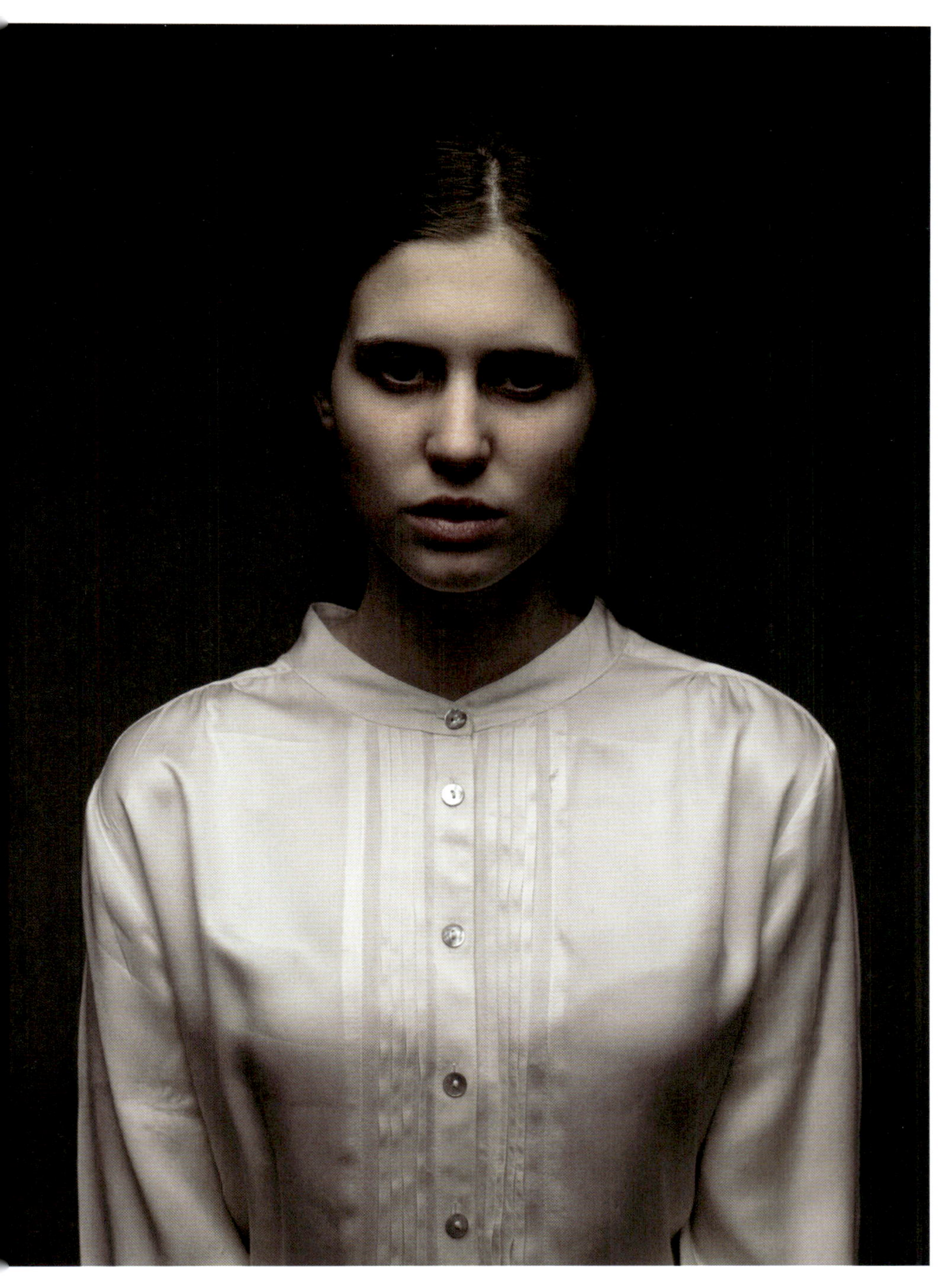

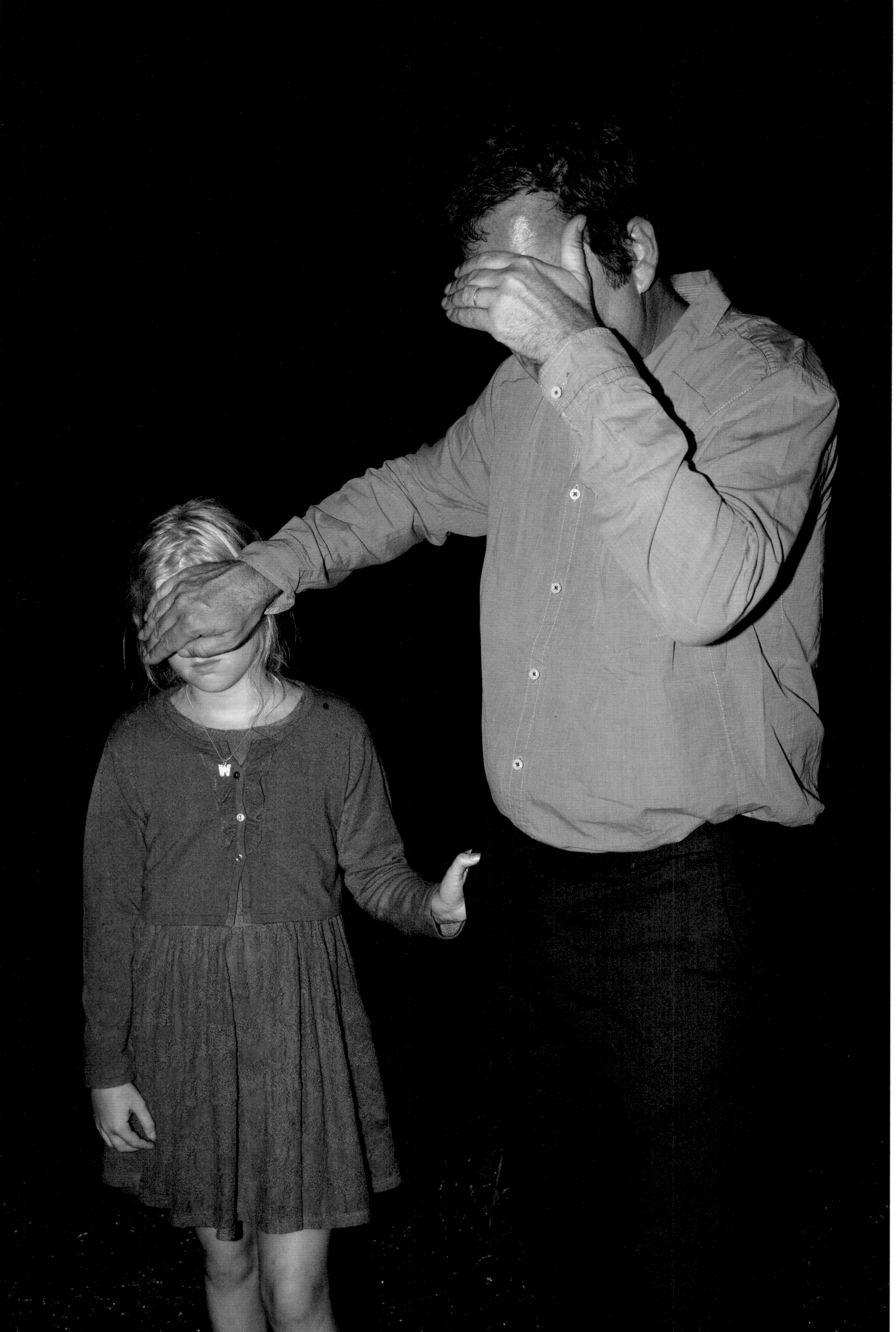

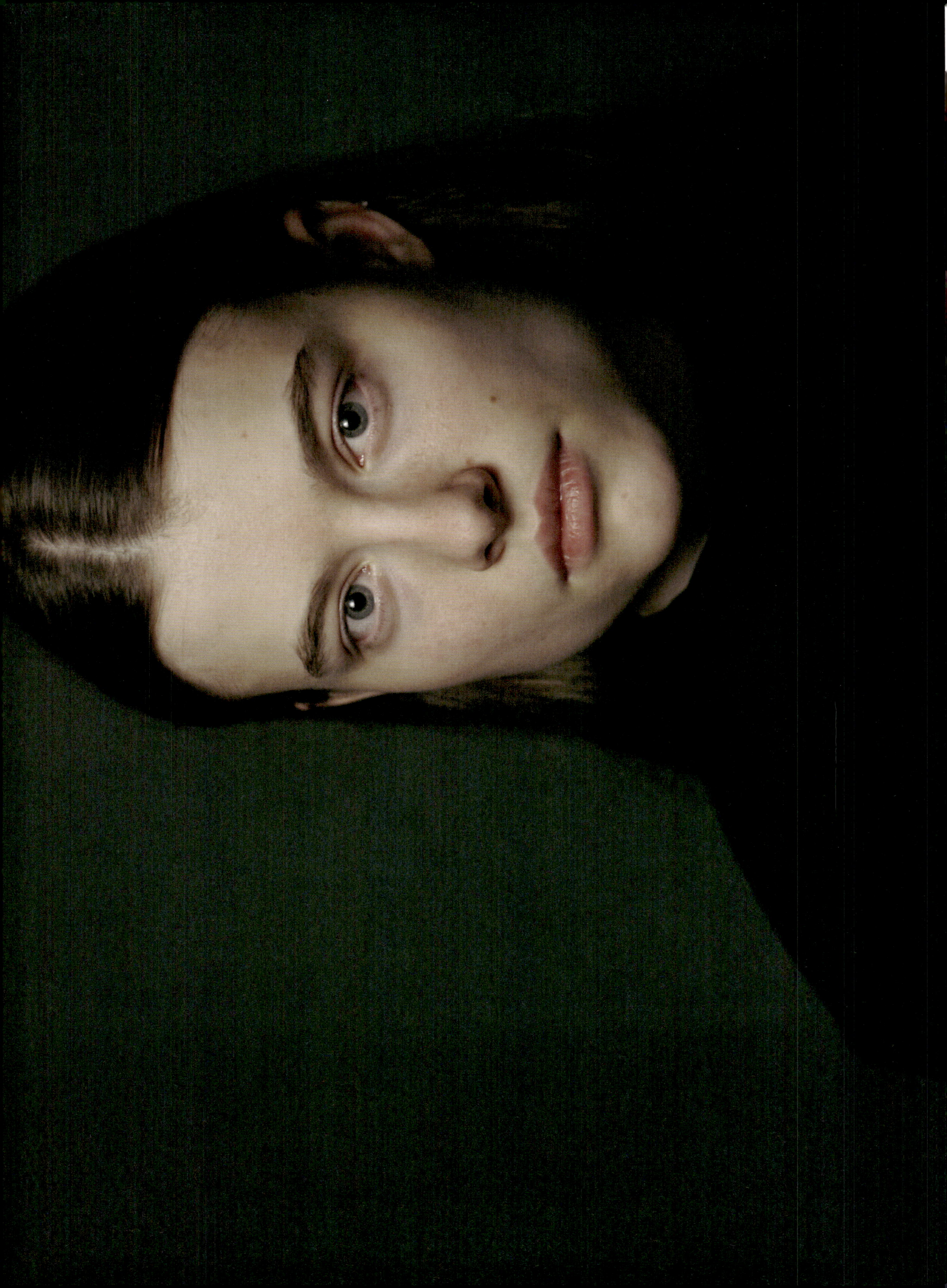

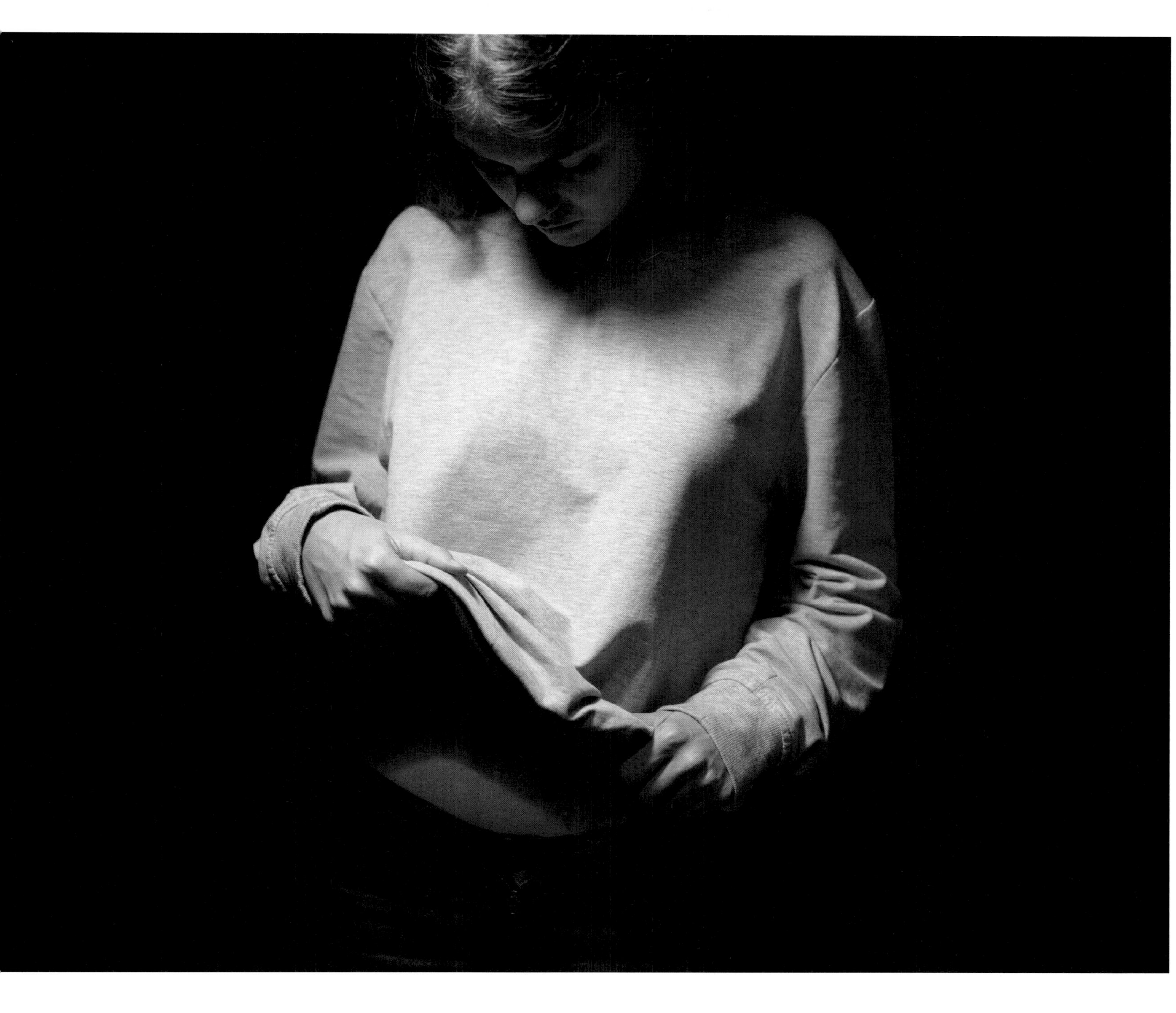

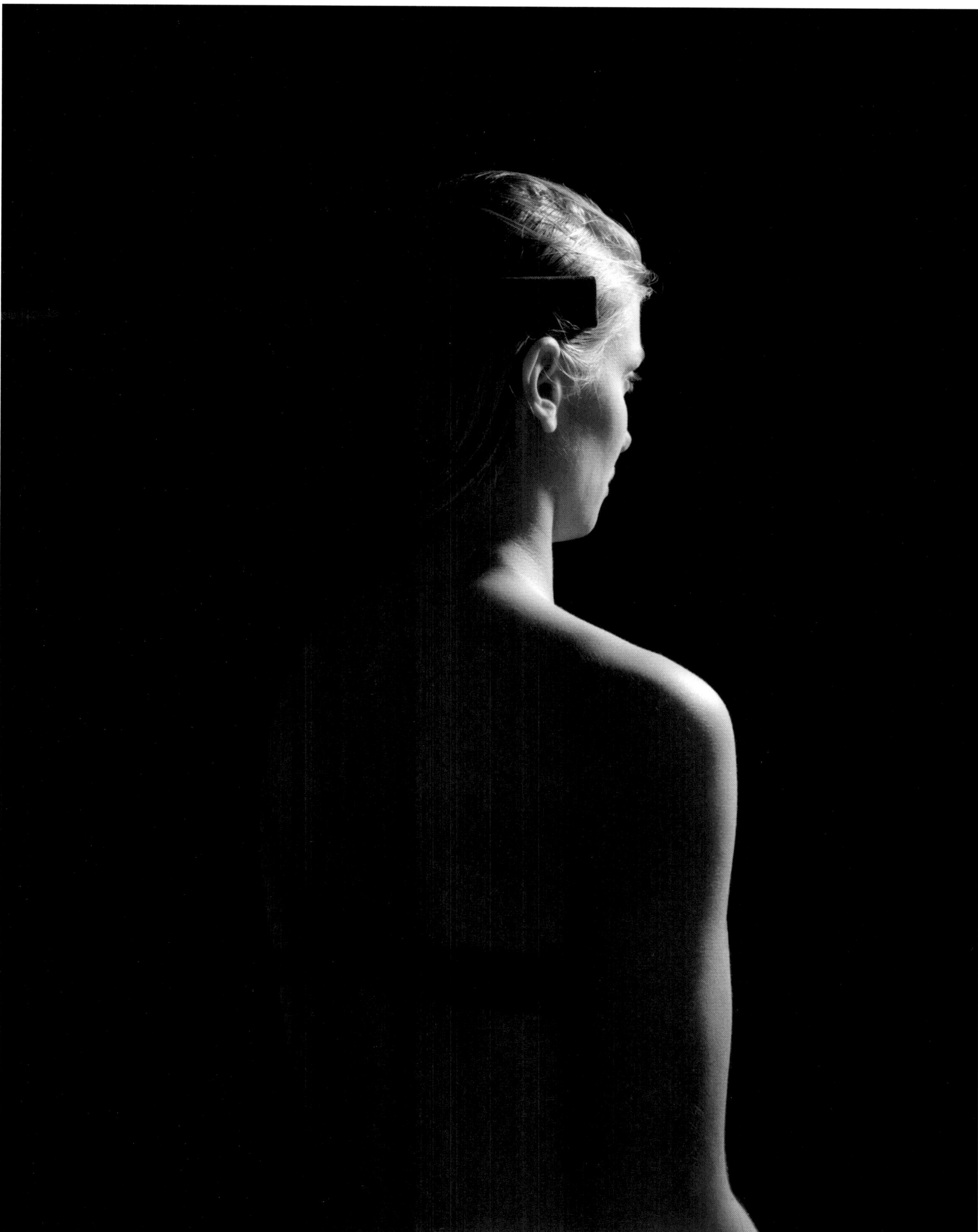

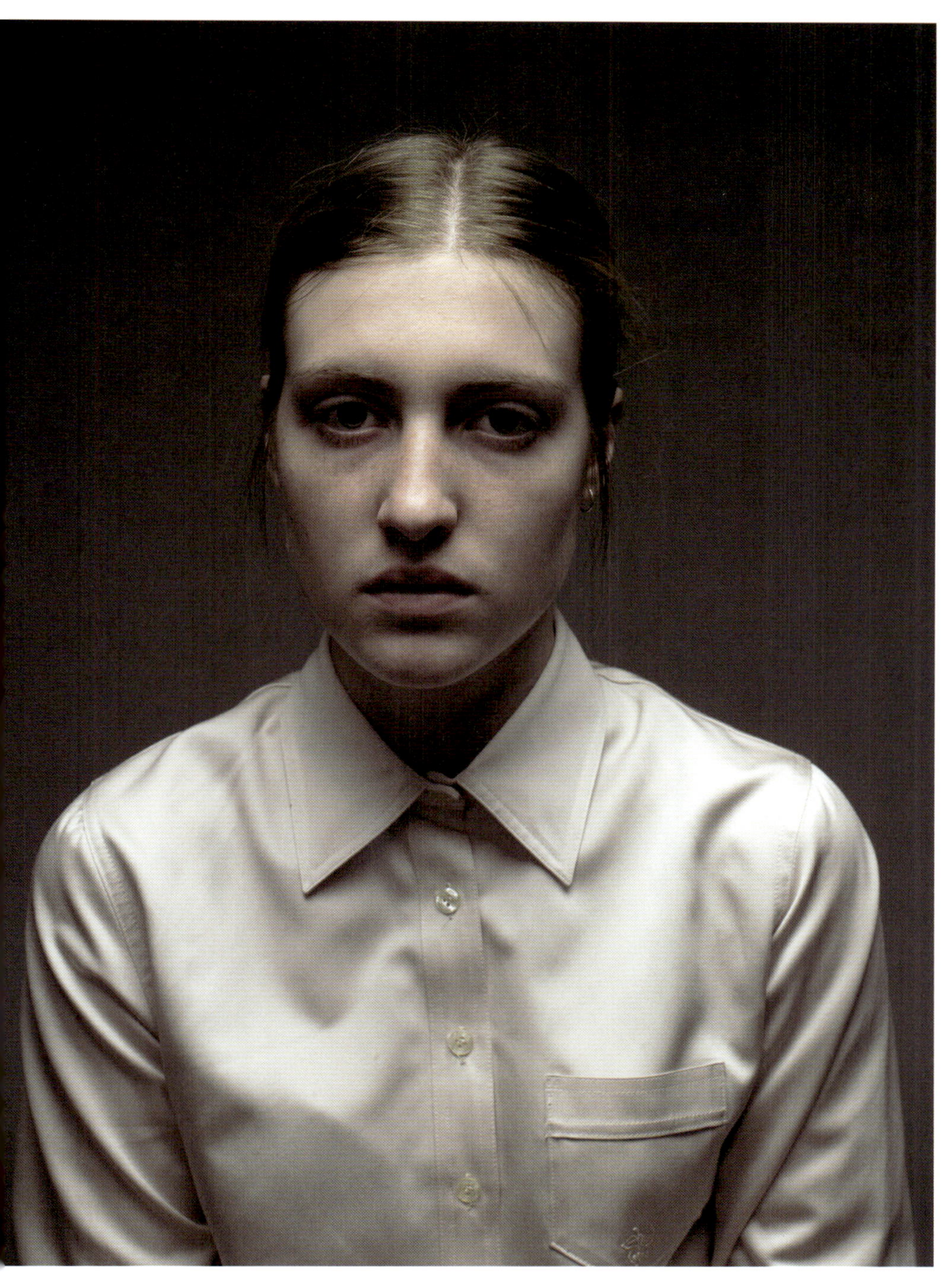

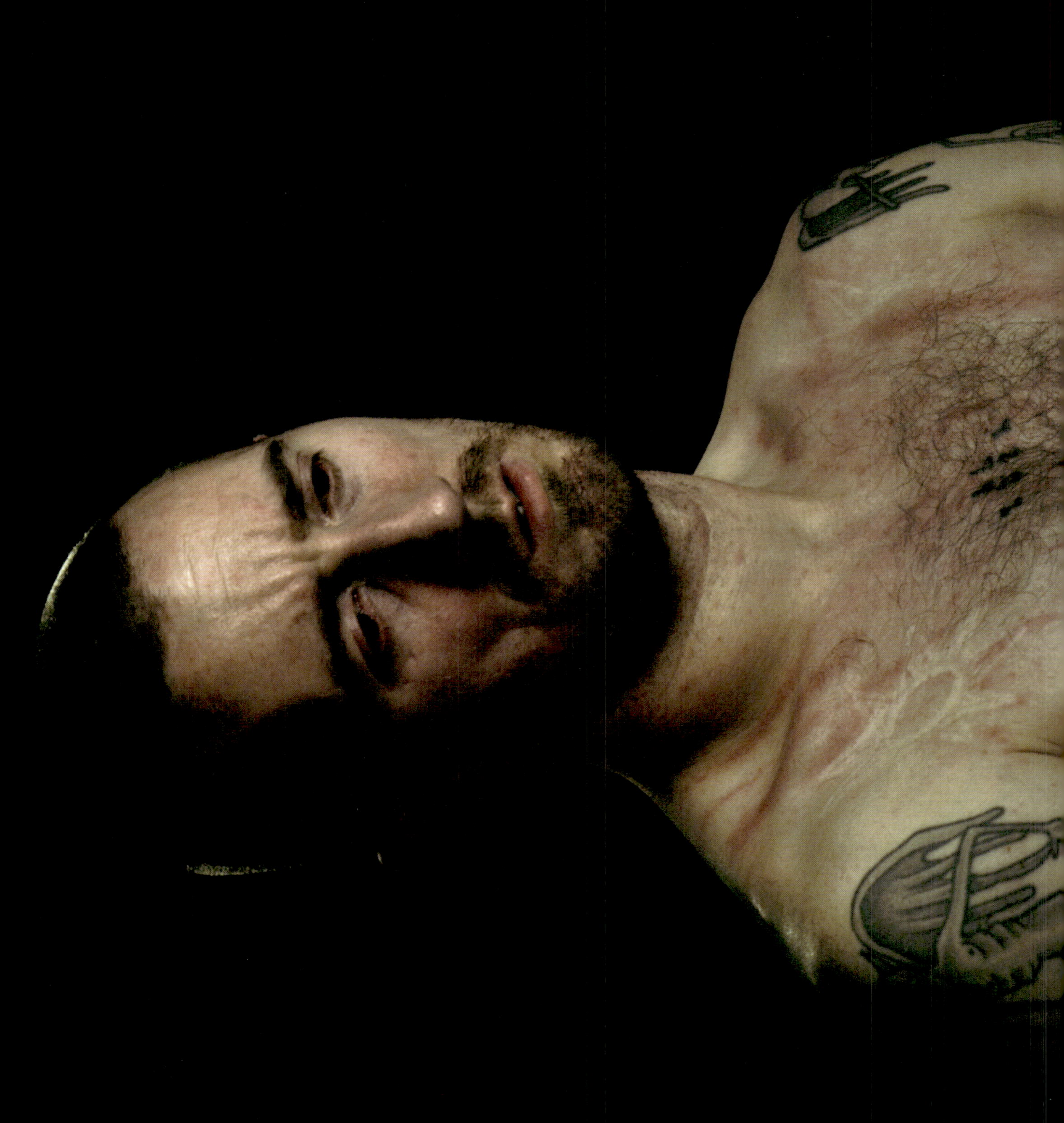

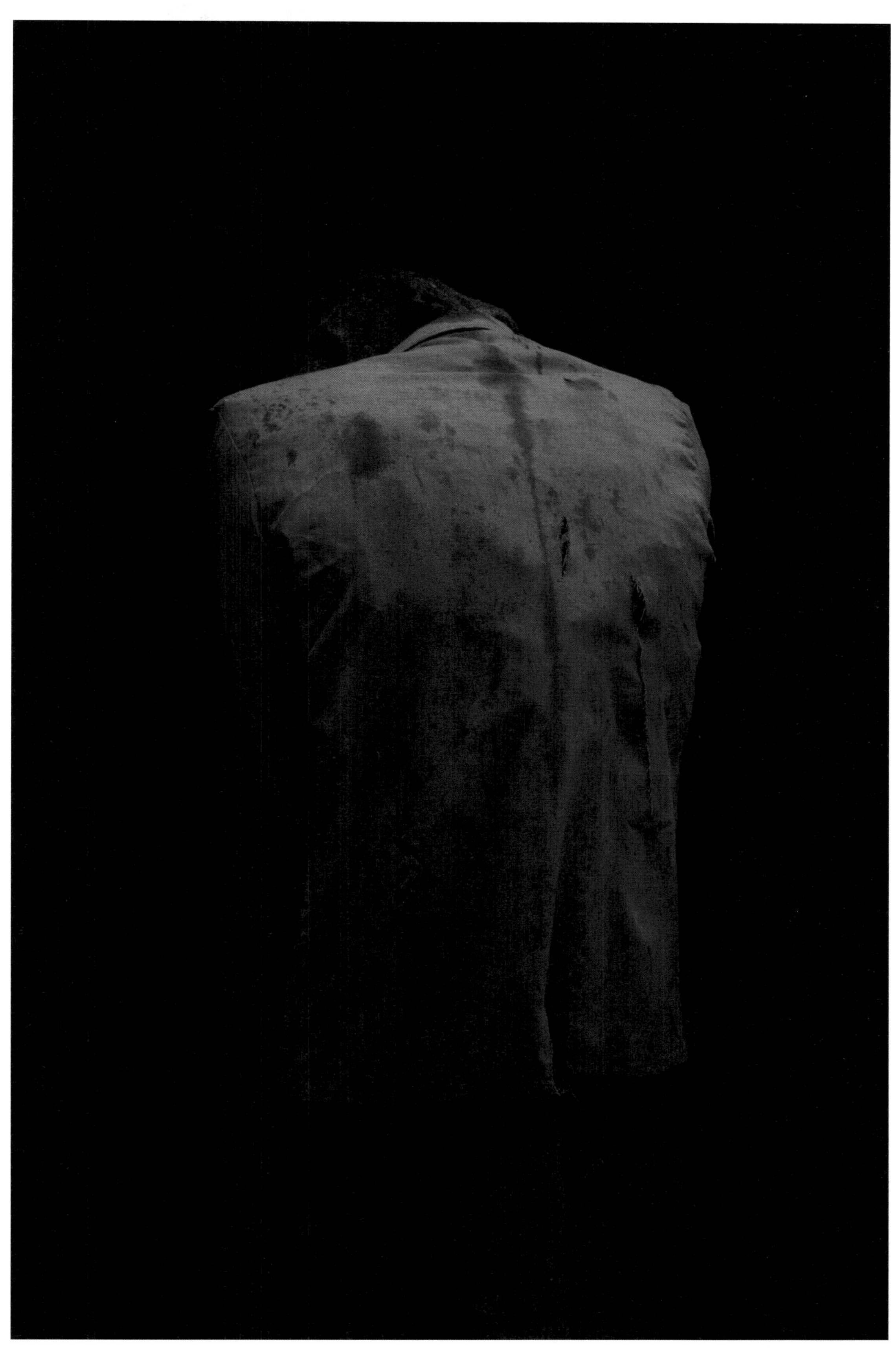

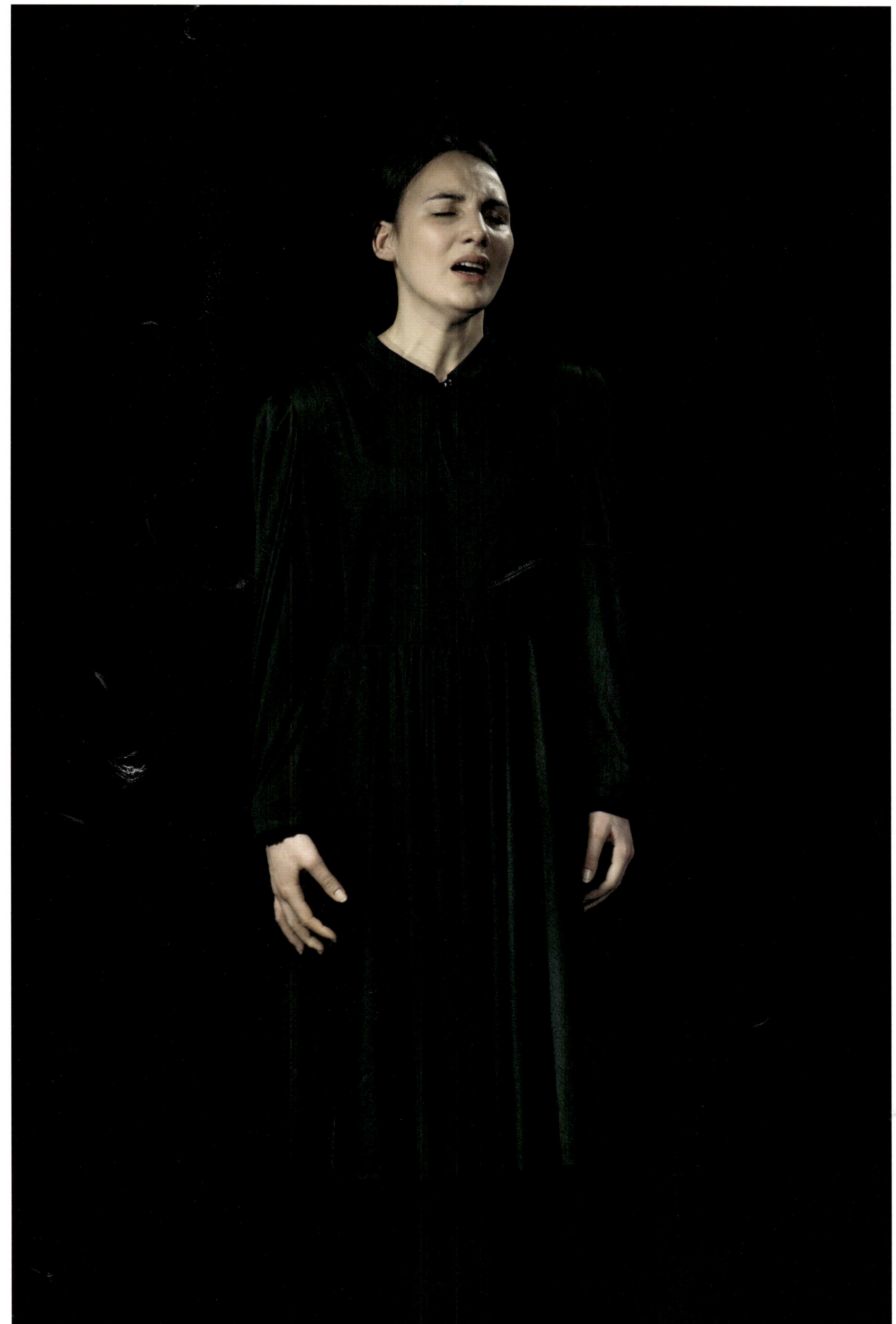

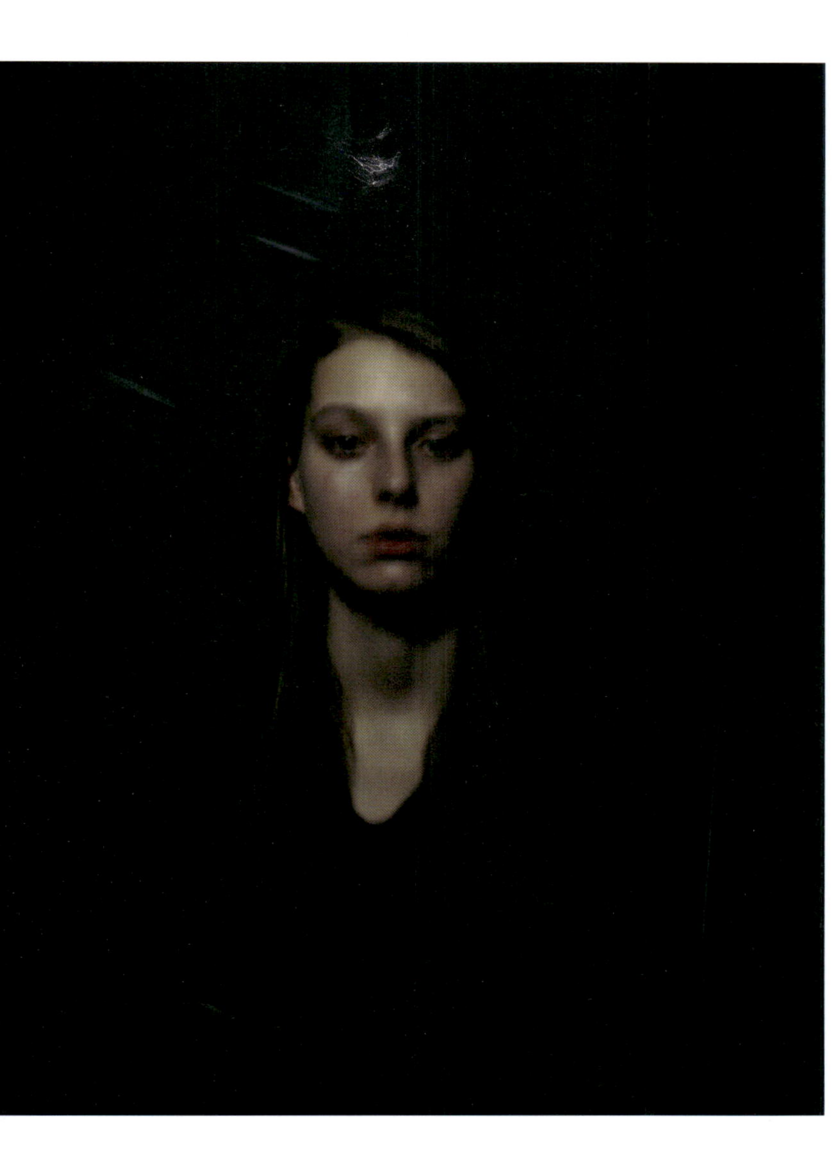

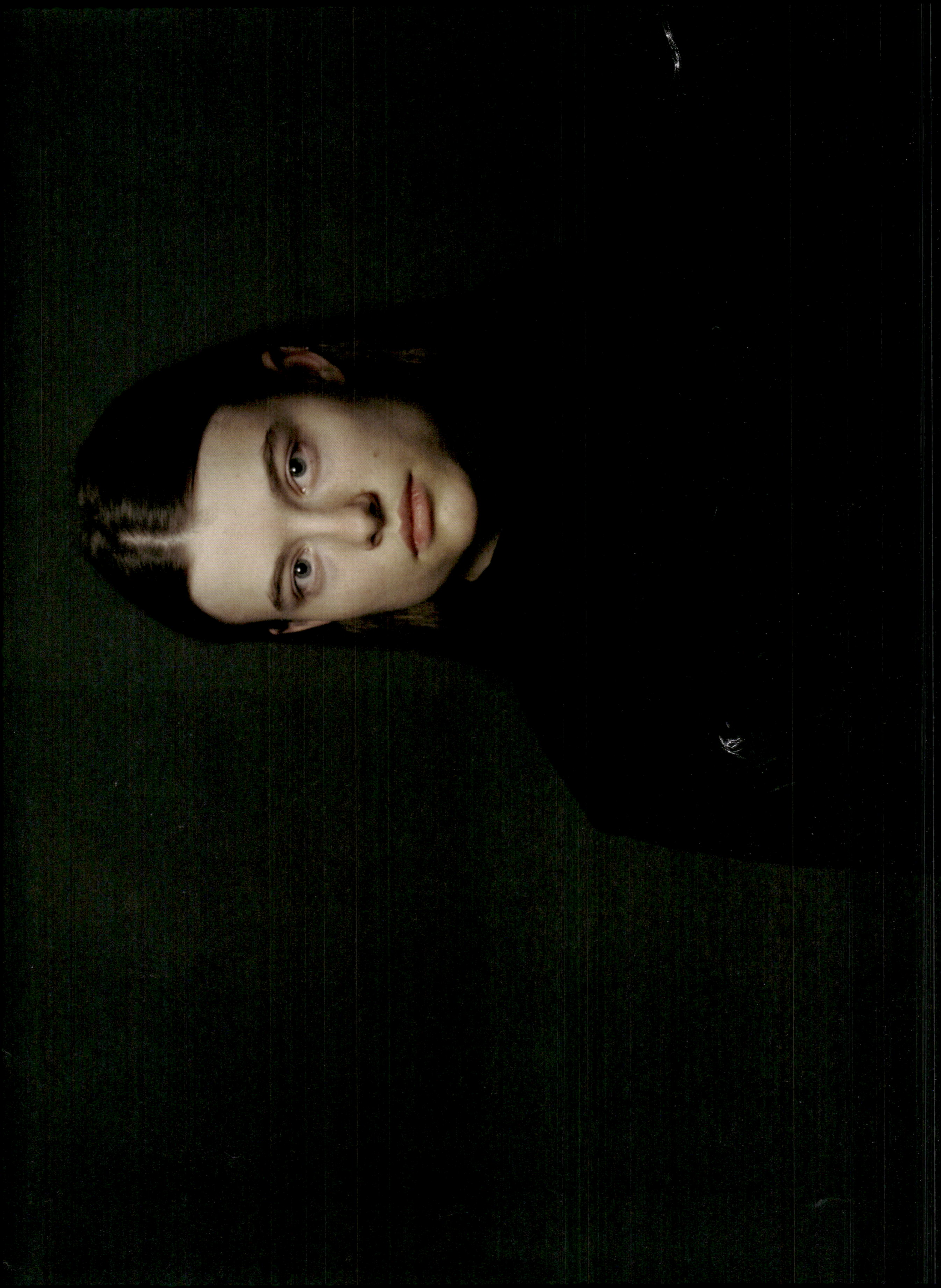

Taco Hidde Bakker

Portrait #5

CONCENTRATION ON 12 MINUTES

Is it true that the photo camera can record what the naked eye can't see? Walter Benjamin named this phenomenon 'the optical unconscious': a photograph not as mere transmission of an image as reflected onto film or sensor by the camera's mirror, but rather a projection of a scientist's vision. Its realisation amounts to an effort to influence coincidence. And in working with live models, chance inevitably seeps in through the cracks. One of his models stated that Callemin provides for a context in which 'freedom is recalled as much as inconvenience, both of which are demanded (or given) by the means of taking photographs – freedom in spite of a measured plan about what the photo should become, because enough space is given to imbue the portrait with something of your own.'

For his photographs without living models, Callemin created models with meticulous care. Nothing may be left to chance. A model also means reduction in size, miniaturisation, a scaling down so artist as well as viewer is in nearly total control, at a distance, with the pleasant illusion of having a better grip on things. The goal of perfection maximises the chances of failure. Callemin: 'I attach so many conditions that it has become almost impossible to realise photographs as I had imagined them beforehand. For me, it's important that an image comes into being exactly as it should be, and I sometimes go to great lengths to arrive at that precise image, although perhaps in the end each image proves to be a failure.'

Working with living models is something else, and involves a different relationship between photographer and subject. Film director Robert Bresson wrote in his collection of aphorisms on cinema, *Notes on Cinematography:* 'The point is not to direct someone, but to direct oneself.'

Bresson demanded of his actors an almost robotic performance, devoid of personality. One way of reaching this is to exhaust your models. In a complex game of mirrors, Bresson must have given his models the feeling they were directing themselves, while they were actually mimicking Bresson directing himself.

The taking of a portrait is tantamount to a delicate act of balancing gazes. Who gazes at whom? From where is the model looking? Looking at...? The gaze turns inward after several minutes, the form of the disappearing photographer perhaps still an afterimage on the retina. What, after all, does the viewer of such a portrait—a face that grows into the image—perceive? Why do these burnt-in faces give such a lasting impression?

What I feel happens over the long duration of ocular concentration is that vision reaches the stage of a seeing that can't be seen. And while other senses press from all sides, vision wants to fold into itself and disappear.

Portrait #5

MEDITATION ON 35 MINUTES

Before you started your experiment in voluntary imprisonment, you made sure to have eaten and to be well-rested, for as you'll soon discover, fixing your face in time demands ultimate concentration. Each compulsion unrestrained will leave its trace in your 35-minute-long face.

It feels like your body has been tacked onto an imaginary cross. You'd like to bow your head, but a power beyond control keeps it in place. As you ascend into focus, the darkened room starts to expand, as vision's other senses begin to prick up their antennae. Are you still sure of what your eyes just saw? Nuances of penumbra reach your mind – your mind starting to flow more easily now that your body releases its tension as it is being fixed in time.

As you feel your forehead heating up, and the buzz in your ears swelling, you think about the difference between recorded time and lived time. You aren't sure any longer whether you are slowly going into limbo or if lived experience is intensifying. The muscles of your neck grow stiff, your throat goes dry, the darkness pulls comfort over your head, yet gives cause to disquietude.

Does recording breach your inborn sense of time? You've promised yourself not to think of the alarm at all, but you feel it is beginning to strike you from all sides. 15 minutes must have passed for sure. For a split second, you are reminded of the presence of a camera and its photographer: it's only role-playing and a role to play. The 35 minutes, in which your mind will reach the highest aperture, is modelling you into a moving portrait. You think of what duration has to endure, how much endurance it takes to be framed by duration. But then the alarm rings much more suddenly. You may put your regular face back on, but have one more answer to find: can justice to this portrait be done only by returning the gaze for as long as it took for this photograph to come into being?

Portrait #2

THE EMPTY HEART

You were sure that hands could see / that which would escape the eye. / Your hands expressing themselves as precisely / and subtly as does your face – its ways of seeing / and sensing things far beyond the grasp / of your eyes, nervously spinning left and right / of your nose; eyes never getting hold of the centre, / the centre your hands possess an unfathomable / ability to encompass.

You had heard that in Japan they don't consider / emptiness to be empty. Essential voids, invisible centres / of gravity, overflowing with detail and meaning, / and given a name reminding you of the place your mother takes in life:

MA

The lines of your hand will be perfectly traced by the camera's uncanny talent / for projecting onto the visible world its own heart – as dark / and impenetrable as the theatre's blackest curtains.

You wonder whether emptiness could be grasped by the hands alone, and / whether the heart could think without the mind.

Portrait #1

FACES IN THE DARK

Left alone under the cloak of darkness, / You and the photographer: a tacit agreement. / The epitome of trust – / A portrait session as question mark?

Enter another dimension within your self / to a nadir of selfhood. / A flash will bring you back, the photographer / acts as your night watchman.

Realities of your body, interface between interior and exterior. / 'If you wish to descend, ascend into the deepest pit' / is what you think you remember, / from a story that wanders around your mind.

Still – with a shock – the flash rends the silence. / Now you are more certain than ever that your face will be faced, / and seen anew with other eyes.

MINIMAL INTRUSION — A continuous portrait burns into film after the photographer has left open the shutter. Forget about his presence, he suggested; focus on your flesh, your breathing and wonder what kind of nothing it is between the camera and you.

MAXIMAL INTRUSION — A continuous portrait burns into the film after the photographer has left open the shutter. You won't get off easy, as a photo camera constantly flashes to hack away your face from the filmic flow; the photographer decides, carries you into the moment in which you'll physically experience the difference between film-time and photo-time.